DRESS
Italian

ISBN 0-9542172-0-9

Printed in Italy, March 2002
by Elcograf a Trade Mark of Pozzoni SPA
Beverate di Brivio (LC) - Italy

First Edition

Published by
Bocca della Verita' Ltd.
22 Wyvil Road
London
SW8 2TG UK
+44 20 7627 0087

DRESS

Italian

51/119
BB.08/02/03

tuscan

WHITE TRUFFLE O

honey

glaze

PRODUCED IN ITALY

'But does it work on pasta?'

Italians enjoy food. They are also masters at infiltrating their way to the front of queues to buy it, without which a trip to Italy would not be complete, or drowning out our conversation when sat next to them in restaurants. They also enjoy talking about it. Endlessly - with some justification it has to be said.

We have a confession to make: so do we!

The Dress Italian Cookbook has been written to accompany our products with the hope of dispelling a question that is most often asked of the range itself: 'But does it work on pasta?'

While we all enjoy pasta - statistics show that it is virtually synonymous with our enjoyment of Italian food - our intention in writing the Cookbook has been, principally, to give greater emphasis to other ways of expressing our ever widening appreciation of Italian food in its entirety.

We hope that the introduction to the recipes themselves also transmit a little historic background, as well as some of our own enthusiasm for the task in both developing, and writing about, the products in the Dress Italian range.

We would like to know your thoughts on the range, recipes and cookbook! You can email us at: thecookbook@dressitalian.com

contents

Dedication

Thank you to Marinetti and Savonarola for dispelling the idea that all Italians love pasta. To Garibaldi for actually being right.

'Is it not enough for you to eat your pasta fried. No! You think you have to add garlic to it, and when you eat ravioli, it is not enough to boil it in a pot and eat it in its juice, you have to fry it in another pot and cover it with cheese!'
Fra Girolamo Savonarola's attempt to ban pasta as evil.
Florence 14th Century

'For heaven's sake, wasn't it time to do something about that barbaric food which had only survived by scrounging off our ultra modern civilisation: I'm speaking of a maccheroni in a sauce, with tomatoes or however you like it. This dish, surely most bestial than any other, looks to us like a female chimpanzee in a sentimental ladies' drawing room.'
F.T. Marinetti
The Futurist Cookbook 1932

'It will be maccheroni. I swear to you, that will unite Italy'
Giuseppe Garibaldi 1860 on the liberation of Naples

Fior d'Olio Organic Extra Virgin Olive Oil

Fior d'Olio Limone Extra Virgin Olive O
with organic lemon

Fior d'Olio Extra Virgin Olive Oil

Clementine Mostarda
Marinade

Vegetable Mostarda
Marinade

Pasticcio di Peperoni

Pear Mostarda
Marinade

Pasticcio di Verdur

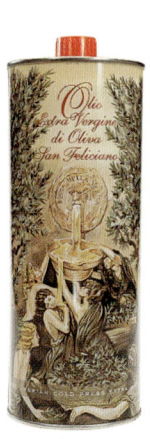

Pasticcio all'Agrodolce

Truffle flavoured Extra Virgin Olive Oil

San Feliciano Extra Virgin Olive Oil

Basil Pesto

Coriander Pesto

Ginger & Parsley Pesto

L'Orientale Dressing

Forcella Dressing

Truffle Honey Glaze

Balsamic Honey Glaze

Rialto Dressing

allaro' Dressing

Salsa Madre

Full range of products may not be available in all stores

involtini di crudo con tomini

baked goat's cheese parcels wrapped with prosciutto

Prosciutto crudo here encloses a triumverate of flavours usually found gracing the cheese board of any self respecting Piedmontese restaurant in the company of one or more of the no less than seven DOP cheeses this region offers. Why wait for the end of the meal when they can be wrapped in prosciutto crudo and enjoyed as a warm appetizer?

Serves 4
Preparation time 10 minutes
Cooking time 15 minutes

4 small goat's crottins (with rind) approx. 60g, 2oz each
4 slices of prosciutto crudo/ Parma ham
4 bay leaves
freshly ground black pepper
4 tsp, 50g, 1/4 cup Dress Italian Truffle Honey Glaze
4 tsp, 20ml, Truffle Flavoured Extra Virgin Olive Oil or Extra Virgin Olive Oil

Preheat the oven to 200 C, 400 F, Gas mark 6

Wrap one slice of prosciutto crudo around each cheese. Place the cheeses on a baking tray, each on top of a bay leaf. Drizzle over Dress Italian Truffle Honey Glaze and Truffle Flavoured Extra Virgin Olive Oil and sprinkle with black pepper.

Place in the oven and bake for 10 minutes.

Remove from the oven and place under a hot grill for 1 minute so they turn golden brown on top.

Serve immediately with toasted Italian bread or crostini as an antipasto.

tortine di formaggio e peperoni

mini goat's cheese tartlets

Singular Italian finger food that can only be referred to in the plural; 'I'll just have one more tortino' is enough to induce a smirk from the most disciplined Italian waiter as if you have unwittingly laid an egg by ordering a baked frittata or omelette! Would madam prefer avocado, goat's cheese and chilli?

Serves 4
Preparation time 20 minutes

24 savoury mini tartlets cases
200g, 7oz, 1 cup fresh goat's cheese
200g, 7oz, 3/4 cup Dress Italian Pasticcio All'Agrodolce
3 tbsp, 45ml, 1 1/2 fl oz extra virgin olive oil
fresh basil leaves, torn
freshly ground black pepper

Fill each tartlet with a small amount of goat's cheese. Spoon Dress Italian Pasticcio all'Agrodolce onto the goat's cheese in each tartlet case. Season with black pepper and drizzle with extra virgin olive oil. Scatter with torn basil leaves and serve.

Serve with chilled Semillon or Pinot Grigio as an aperitif.

sfizio di crudo con cresenza
ham & cheese wrap

Snacks or *sfizi* come in all shapes and sizes. The tangy sweet flavour of *crescenza* contrasts pleasantly with the inherent blandness of most bread wraps, while complementing a wide variety of other ingredients such as prosciutto, olives and pears. When heated, crescenza is even more delicious, but it 'runs'. You have been warned!

Serves 4
Preparation time 15 minutes

4 large sandwich wraps
12 slices of prosciutto crudo/Parma ham
100g, 4oz, 1/2 cup crescenza or fresh cream cheese
100g, 4oz, 3 cups of loosely packed lambs lettuce
4 tbsp, 60g, 1/4 cup Dress Italian L'Orientale Dressing
salt and black pepper

Toss the lambs lettuce with Dress Italian L'Orientale Dressing in a large bowl and season with salt and pepper.

Open flat each wrap and spread with crescenza or cream cheese. Add three slices of prosciutto crudo to each wrap and top with the dressed lambs lettuce.

Roll up each wrap and slice into 4 pieces.

Serve with a salad or as a snack.

Coda:
Ideal as a picnic snack or cut into smaller pieces as an appetiser.

insalata d'orzo mediterranea
barley, pesto & tomato salad

Barley is eaten throughout northern Italy, particularly in Friuli Venezia Giulia. Used with herbs, broad beans, smoked pancetta, sautéed wild mushrooms and winter vegetables it offers up delightful soups and risotto style dishes called *orzata*. It works equally well as an *insalata* or appetizer, here seen in the company of sunnier Italian ingredients.

Serves 4
Preparation time 10 minutes
Cooking time 25 minutes

250g, 8oz, 1 cup pearl barley
250g, 8oz, 1¹/2 cups chopped cherry tomatoes
1 clove of garlic, finely chopped
3 tbsp, 50g, ¹/4 cup Dress Italian Basil Pesto
4 tbsp, 60ml, 2fl oz extra virgin olive oil
fresh basil leaves, torn
salt and black pepper
a few pine nuts

Rinse the pearl barley under cold water until the water runs clear. Boil the pearl barley until 'al dente' (approximately 25 minutes). Drain and rinse under cold water.

Mix the cooled barley with the chopped tomatoes, olive oil, pesto, garlic and torn basil leaves. Season with salt and pepper and scatter with pine nuts.

Stir well and serve.

Coda:
For a tangier flavour, stir through the juice of half a lemon. The flavour of this salad is enhanced by making the dish a day in advance, covered then stored, in the refrigerator.

glazes

Let's not knock sugar.

It doesn't warrant an entry in the index of any cookery book, because, due to its ubiquitous presence we take it both for granted and consider it unworthy of mention. Yet just how successful it was when introduced into western Europe and why, makes for interesting reading.

Sugar supplied a much cheaper alternative to honey as a preservative and a sweetener with a less intrusive aftertaste that lent itself less temperamentally to use as a cooking ingredient. The neutral background flavour of sugar also, in part, contributed to the growing habit of writing down recipes with the specific objective of sharing them with readers, who for the first time could imagine the overall taste of a recipe without the extra complication of finding a honey to replace the inevitably regionally produced and locally available one cited in the original.

While sugar was not a universal replacement for honey - consider its use as an accompaniment to cheese of which the Piedmontese are particularly partial to this day - it did continue to supply the benchmark against which the usefulness of honey was judged. Basting roasts could be a problem with granulated sugar.

Hold that thought!

Consider the case of Balsamic vinegar. Rather than create a thick sauce by either gradually reducing the liquid to a syrup or thickening with flour, when combined instead with honey it achieves a thick flavoursome sauce in a fraction of the time and to better effect. The same can be said for black or white truffle oil, porcini mushrooms and beyond. Imagine a Sicillian orange scented honey mixed with Marsala wine and pistaccio nuts, for instance. Suddenly the thought that honey can become a legitimate vehicle for introducing a touch of regional authenticity to your Italian dishes takes hold.

Sounds innovative? Yet the ancient Romans loved honeys flavoured with the likes of mint, rosemary, coriander, fennel and celery seeds and passed on their delight in the combination of sweet and savoury flavours, to which honey, of course, lends itself, to subsequent generations. Would the Arabic delight in agro dolce achieved through the use of lemons, almonds and sultanas, have been so readily absorbed into Italian culture without the precedent set by the Ancient Romans? Stirring stuff!

insalata di bresaola parmigiano e rucola

bresaola salad with rocket and shaved parmesan

Here's a starter that's a perennial favourite with north Italian restaurant goers, and it's easy to understand why. It teases and satisfies the palate while resting easy on the stomach; it doesn't require constant eye contact in order to eat safely and one isn't going to be accused of being more interested in the menu than in the company one keeps!

Serves 4
Preparation time 15 minutes

16 slices of bresaola
100g, 4oz, 2 cups fresh wild rocket
75g, 3oz, 3/4 cup Parmigiano Reggiano shavings
juice of 1 lemon
4 tsp, 50g, 1/4 cup Dress Italian Truffle Honey Glaze
4 tbsp, 60ml, 2 fl oz extra virgin olive oil
salt and freshly ground black pepper

Arrange four slices of bresaola on each plate. Squeeze the juice of the lemon over the bresaola.

Toss the rocket with the extra virgin olive oil. Season with salt and pepper and place on top of the bresaola. Sprinkle over the Parmigiano Reggiano shavings and drizzle each plate with Dress Italian Truffle Honey Glaze. Season with black pepper.

Serve with fresh crusty bread as a starter or as a light lunch.

caponata magra
baked aubergines with forcella dip

Rather than frying cubed aubergines, onions, celery and tomato pulp in olive oil before adding sugar, vinegar and olives, as dictated by the original sweet & sour Sicilian recipe, aubergines are instead baked and mixed with Forcella dressing that itself contains pine nuts, sultanas, olives and white wine vinegar. Add capers & tomatoes to taste.

Serves 4
Preparation time 10 minutes
Cooking time approx. 40 minutes

2 aubergines (eggplants) cut in half lengthways
4 tbsp, 60ml, 2fl oz extra virgin olive oil
3 tbsp, 60g, 1/4 cup Dress Italian Forcella Dressing
20 pitted black olives
salt and pepper
4 cherry tomatoes

Preheat oven to 220 C, 425 F, Gas mark 7

Place the aubergines, flesh side down onto a baking tray and drizzle with 1 tbsp of oil. Place in the oven and bake for 40 minutes or until the skin is blackened and the flesh is soft.

Scoop the flesh out away from the skin and allow to cool. Chop the cooled aubergine flesh into small pieces and combine with the Dress Italian Forcella Dressing.

Slice the olives and add to the chopped aubergine together with the remaining olive oil. Season with salt and pepper to taste.

Garnish with cherry tomatoes cut in half and serve with vegetable crudités and fresh crusty bread.

Coda:
Add capers, sugar and vinegar to recreate the original Arabic inspired sweet & sour taste.

polpette di carne con pasticcio di peperoni
mini burgers with pasticcio di peperoni

Sicilian polpette are alternating portions of meatballs and small round slices of white bread on a skewer, pan fried & served with a side sauce of lemon, garlic and parsley. Why not instead serve them hamburger style dressed with a peperonata instead of 'ketchup' as finger food? Even the use of sesame seeds on buns is reminiscent of the decoration on Sicilian *mafalda* bread.

Serves 4
Preparation time 40 minutes
Cooking time 15 minutes

8 small mini bread rolls
8 mini hamburger patties (see Coda below)
5 tbsp, 125g, 1/2 cup Dress Italian Pasticcio di Peperoni
60g, 2oz, 1 cup lambs lettuce
salt and pepper
1 tbsp extra virgin olive oil
sunflower oil for frying

Lightly toast the mini bread rolls.

Pan fry the mini hamburger patties in sunflower oil for 4 minutes and pat dry with kitchen paper. Toss the lambs lettuce with the extra virgin olive oil and season with salt and pepper.

Assemble each burger bun with a mini pattie, topped with lambs lettuce and a generous dollop of Dress Italian Pasticcio di Peperoni.

Serve immediately.

Coda:
Use the meatball recipe from 'Timballo di melanzane con polpette' on page 83 to make your hamburger patties.

frittata di peperoni
Italian flat omelette with red and yellow peppers

An Italian omelette or *frittata* can be prepared impromptu, cut into small squares and offered as an antipasto, served as a light lunch or used to fill a sandwich. It can be purchased ready made in good salumerie where they resemble thick flat pancakes that have been well cooked on both sides and crammed with ingredients.

Serves 4
Preparation time 10 minutes
Cooking time 20 minutes

8 large eggs
1 jar, 280g Dress Italian Pasticcio di Peperoni
50g, 2 oz, 1/3 cup Parmigiano Reggiano freshly grated
salt and black pepper
2 tbsp, 50g, 1/4 cup single cream
2 tbsp, 60 ml, 2fl oz extra virgin olive oil

Preheat the oven to 220 C, 425 F, Gas mark 7

Beat together the eggs, cream, salt, pepper and Parmigiano Reggiano until combined. Pour Dress Italian Pasticcio di Peperoni into the mixture, stir well and pour into a well greased terracotta baking dish.

Bake in a preheated oven for 15 minutes or until the frittata is firm to the touch and browned on top.

Cut into large pieces and serve with salad or as part of a brunch or lunch.

Coda:
Serve at room temperature, cut into small bite sized pieces as an appetiser or refrigerate overnight and serve cold.

pan pizza con gorgonzola e rucola

pizza with rocket & gorgonzola

The trick here is that the pizza base is fully cooked before the topping is added thereby providing a biscuit consistency that more easily supports the rocket salad, *gorgonzola*, walnut and truffle honey dressing. It can be safely cut into thin wedges and served as an appetizer.

Serves 4
Preparation time 10 minutes
Cooking time approx. 10 minutes

2 plain pizza bases
100g, 4oz, 2 cups fresh wild rocket
120g, 5oz, 1 cup gorgonzola or stilton cheese cut into cubes
1 tbsp Dress Italian Truffle Honey Glaze
salt and freshly ground black pepper
30g, 1oz, 1/3 cup walnuts
2 tbsp, 30ml, 1fl oz extra virgin olive oil
2 tbsp, 30ml, 1fl oz truffle flavoured oil

Preheat the oven to 220 C, 425 F, Gas mark 7.

Bake the pizza bases for about 5-7 minutes until hot and crunchy. Meanwhile, toss the rocket in a bowl with the extra virgin olive oil and truffle oil. Season with salt and pepper.

Remove the pizza bases from the oven. Place the seasoned rocket on each pizza and sprinkle the gorgonzola and walnuts onto the rocket. Drizzle with the Dress Italian Truffle Honey Glaze and serve with a chilled glass of dry white wine.

Can be served as an accompaniment to pre-dinner drinks or as a sophisticated starter.

salsa

The tomato, now aged 461, started its recorded life in the Old World as a condiment for meats and fish.

Its first mention in Naples dates from 1692 as *Salsa di Pomodoro alla spagnola*. Yet while the title cocks a polite hat towards the Spanish Bourbon dynasty then ruling over Naples, the recipe itself suggests the beginnings of a product that would eventually re-emerge in the New World - as Ketchup.

By the 1780s, the Tomato was being used in many of the 60 or so courses served as part of a banquet 'in the French manner'. Its contribution, however, was limited to that of a coulis, or reduction, prepared by boiling fresh tomatoes in a meat broth until reduced to a paste that would then be added in small amounts to various recipes.

And so it might have continued had it not been for a Frenchman named Appert, who by 1810 perfected a process of vacuuming food in order to preserve it - an invention we celebrate every time we open a tin of food.

The impact on the status of tomatoes was immediate. *Concentrato di Pomodoro* emerged for the first time to offer chefs a ready made substitute to having to make a coulis each time from scratch: it contained no animal fat residues, it could be stored at room temperature - fridges did not yet exist - and more importantly for our story, it cost a fraction of the price to produce.

The new technology led to an export generated boom in tomatoes and its derivatives that Neapolitans were quick to exploit for their own food as well - by using it on pasta. When you consider that pasta, before then, had been dressed with an Arab influenced mixture of grated cheese, cinnamon and sugar, you'll understand the attraction!

pappardelle al pomodoro con pinoli

pasta with tomato 'salsa madre' & roasted pine nuts

Originally, tomatoes were sundried in the summer in order to preserve them as a source of food during the winter months. Ligurian *salsa di pomodori secchi* is just such a sauce, prepared with the addition of extra virgin olive oil and pine nuts. Here's a summer version using whole fresh tomatoes that Neapolitans would readily endorse.

Serves 4
Preparation time 10 minutes
Cooking time 10 minutes

400g, 14oz egg pappardelle pasta
1 jar Dress Italian Salsa Madre
fresh basil leaves
30g, 1 oz, 1/4 cup pine nuts, toasted
salt and black pepper
2 tbsp, 30ml, 1fl oz extra virgin olive oil
Parmigiano Reggiano, freshly grated
1 small red chilli, finely chopped (optional)

Heat the olive oil with half of the fresh basil, pine nuts and chilli (optional). Sauté for 1 minute. Add Dress Italian Salsa Madre and cook through for about 2 minutes and remove from the heat.

Add the pappardelle to a large saucepan of boiling salted water and cook for 4 minutes or until *al dente*. Drain the pasta and add it to the Dress Italian Salsa Madre sauce. Toss well.

Add the remaining basil leaves and sprinkle with freshly grated Parmigiano Reggiano. Season with salt and pepper and serve immediately.

pilaf di riso con funghi e verdure

pilaf rice with porcini mushooms

Armenian immigrants brought a tradition for making pilaf rice to Venice that survives to the present day. Its immediate advantage over the preparation of risotto is the use of long grain rather than Arborio or Canaroli rice and the added convenience of being able to add stock all at once rather than gradually, which can be a lifesaver when strapped for time.

Serves 4
Preparation time 10 minutes
Cooking time 20 minutes

400g, 14oz, 1³/₄ cups long grain white rice
1 red onion, finely chopped
10 tbsp, 230g, 1 cup Dress Italian Pasticcio di Verdure
50g, 2oz, 4 tbsp, ¹/₈ cup butter
4 tbsp, 60ml, 2fl oz extra virgin olive oil
small bunch of parsley, finely chopped
50g, 2oz, ¹/₈ cup Parmigiano Reggiano, freshly grated
50g, 2oz dry porcini mushrooms
salt and freshly ground black pepper
2 bay leaves

First soak the porcini mushrooms in a cup of warm water for 15 minutes. Drain and retain the water for later.

Sauté the onion with half of the butter and half of the extra virgin olive oil plus the 2 bay leaves. When the onion is soft and transparent, add Dress Italian Pasticcio di Verdure and the drained porcini mushrooms and cook for a few minutes more.

Boil the rice for about 8 minutes and when still very al dente, drain and add to the pan. Cook together over a medium flame.

Now add the water from the porcini mushrooms and cook for another 4-5 minutes. Add the remaining butter and oil and season with salt and pepper. Finally sprinkle with the Parmigiano Reggiano and chopped parsley and serve immediately.

brodetto di pesce al modo mio
Adriatic seafood broth

Brodetto speaks to us of the Adriatic, of numerous sleepy fishing ports, where the recipe for fish stew has remained a point of historical difference within a landscape of shared flatness. The rare omission of tomatoes here favours Venetian precedence, while the inclusion of herbs and in particular, chilli, suggests an affinity with the Abruzzi region of Italy.

Serves 4
Preparation time 10 minutes
Cooking time 20 minutes

250g, 9oz, 1 cup shelled tiger prawns
170g, 6oz, 1/2 cup flaked cooked or tinned crab
1 clove of garlic, finely chopped
2 small red chillis, finely chopped
3 tbsp, 50g, 1/4 cup Dress Italian Coriander pesto
2 tbsp, 30 ml, 1fl oz extra virgin olive oil
1200 ml, 2 pints, 5 cups cold water
fresh coriander and mint
100g, 1 cup bean sprouts

Heat the extra virgin olive oil with the garlic and chilli in a heavy based frying pan or wok. Sauté for 3 minutes.

Add the prawns, crab meat and Dress Italian Coriander Pesto. Stir well. Pour over the water and simmer gently for about 15 minutes. Add the bean sprouts and season with salt and black pepper.

Sprinkle with fresh coriander and mint and serve immediately.

lasagne con caponata di verdure e zafferano

lasagne with vegetables and saffron sauce

This fusion of antipasto vegetables in the style of a Sicilian *caponata* in place of a meat ragù, together with layered fresh sheets of pasta and *besciamella* sauce, makes for a credible and delicious alternative to the classic offering from Bologna.

Serves 4
Preparation time 20 minutes
Cooking time 40 minutes

8 fresh egg lasagne sheets, boiled and drained
500ml, 16 fl oz Béchamel sauce (see Glossary for recipe)
100g, 4oz, $^1/_3$ cup unsalted butter
salt and black pepper
freshly grated nutmeg
1 white onion, finely chopped
1 jar, 280g Dress Italian Pasticcio di Verdure
4 tbsp, 60 ml, 2fl oz extra virgin olive oil
2 tsp fresh parsley, chopped
75g, $2^1/_2$ oz, $^1/_4$ cup Parmigiano Reggiano, freshly grated
150ml, 5fl oz, $^1/_4$ pint single cream
3 threads, 0.25g of saffron

Preheat oven to 240 C, 450 F, Gas mark 8

Sauté the chopped onion with extra virgin olive oil for a few minutes until the onion is soft and transparent. Add Dress Italian Pasticcio di Verdure and the fresh parsley, stir well and season with salt and black pepper.
After 2 minutes, remove from the heat and set to one side. Add half of the butter together with salt, black pepper and a sprinkle of nutmeg to the Béchamel sauce. Finally fold in 30g of Parmigiano Reggiano. Stir well.

Cover the bottom of a terracotta baking dish with a fine layer of Dress Italian Pasticcio di Verdure. Place 4 sheets of lasagne to cover. Then cover the lasagne with Dress Italian Pasticcio di Verdure and top with half of the Béchamel sauce and sprinkle with half of the remaining Parmigiano Reggiano. Add another layer and top with small knobs of butter placed randomly. Bake in the pre heated oven for 35 minutes. Meanwhile, bring the single cream to a simmer, stir in the saffron and remove from the heat. Season well with salt and pepper. After 25 minutes, open the oven door and pour the saffron sauce over the lasagne. Bake for a further 10 minutes.

Remove from the oven and leave to rest for at least 10 minutes before serving.

risotto finto ai frutti di mare
seafood risotto

Rice Italian style is usually prepared as a *risotto*, although there is a tradition for *pilaf* in Venice inherited from Armenia (see page 36). *Finto* means 'mock' or 'pretend' such as in Neapolitan *sugo finto* where meat is replaced by cheaper pork fat. Here it's just about finding a way of creating something equally delicious in less time.

Serves 4
Preparation time 15 minutes
Cooking time approx. 25 minutes

350g, 10^1/$_2$ oz, 1^1/$_2$ cups long grain white rice
400g, 14oz, 2 cups mixed seafood (shelled mussels, shrimps, prawns, crab, scallops)
1 clove of garlic, finely chopped
^{1}/$_2$ white onion, finely chopped
a handful of flat leaf or continental parsley
4 tbsp, 60ml, 2fl oz extra virgin olive oil
6 fresh mint leaves
3 tbsp, 60g, ^{1}/$_4$ cup Dress Italian Rialto Dressing
3 threads, 0.25g saffron

Cook the rice in a pan of salted boiling water for about 14 minutes or until *al dente*. In a separate pan, heat 3 tbsp of extra virgin olive oil with the garlic and chopped onion. Sauté for 2 minutes or until the onion has softened and is transparent and then add the seafood. Sauté for a further 5 minutes, season with salt and black pepper then add the saffron and pour over Dress Italian Rialto Dressing. Cook for one more minute.

Drain the rice and stir it into the seafood sauce. Season with salt and pepper and stir well. Sprinkle with freshly chopped mint and parsley and drizzle over the remaining extra virgin olive oil.

Remove from the heat and serve immediately.

43

zuppa di carote al marsala
carrot, ginger and marsala soup

Taken from a classic Sicilian recipe for sliced carrots, which includes the unusual recommendation to use butter for sautéing, the inclusion of marsala hints at the more overtly sweet and sour Jewish Venetian *carote alla giudia* with its use of vinegar, nuts and raisins here re-introduced in the form of a ginger and parsley pesto.

Serves 4
Preparation time 20 minutes
Cooking time 30 minutes

500g, 1lb, 3 $^1/_2$ cups carrots
360ml, 12fl oz, 1$^1/_2$ pint carrot water
50g, 2oz, $^1/_4$ cup butter
juice of 1 lemon
4 tbsp, 120g, $^1/_2$ cup crème fraîche
salt and black pepper
4 tsp, 50g, $^1/_4$ cup Dress Italian Ginger & Parsley Pesto
2 tbsp,1fl oz, $^1/_8$ cup Marsala or medium sweet sherry

Peel and cut the carrots into medium sized chunks and boil in salted water for about 15 minutes until soft. Drain the carrots and set aside 568ml (1 pint) of the water. Mash the carrots until smooth using a mouli grinder.

Melt the butter in a pan and add the mashed carrots. Sauté for 2 minutes being careful not to brown and add the retained carrot water. Simmer gently for a further 8 minutes.

Season with salt, black pepper and lemon juice. Add the Marsala and stir well. Serve in individual bowls with a dollop of crème fraîche and one of Dress Italian Ginger & Parsley Pesto.

strangolapreti al pomodoro

potato gnocchi with fresh tomato sauce & crème fraîche

Tomatoes and potato gnocchi form an anti clerical alliance. Pellegrino Artusi relates the story of an over zealous priest nicknamed *Don Pomodoro* who, like the ubiquitous tomato, was to be found everywhere. One almost suspects Neapolitans of having invented these small gnocchi - literally meaning 'priest stranglers' - as an antidote.

Serves 4

Preparation time 25 minutes
Cooking time 20 minutes

400g, 14oz potato gnocchi
1 jar Dress Italian Salsa Madre
20g, 1oz, 1 cup (loosely packed) dry porcini mushrooms
1/2 red onion, finely chopped
50g, 4 tbsp, 2oz butter
4 tbsp, 60ml, 2 fl oz extra virgin olive oil
4 tbsp, 50g, 1/4 cup crème fraîche
salt and freshly ground black pepper
50g, 2oz, 1/4 cup Parmigiano Reggiano, freshly grated

Soak the mushrooms in warm water for at least 20 minutes. Drain and pour away the stock.

Heat the extra virgin olive oil in a pan with the chopped onion until soft and transparent. Add the mushrooms and cook for two minutes. Add Dress Italian Salsa Madre and cook for a further two minutes until heated through. Season with salt and pepper.

Cook the gnocchi in plenty of boiling salted water until they float to the surface. Lift out with a slotted spoon and add to the Dress Italian Salsa Madre sauce. Stir well. Add the butter, Parmigiano Reggiano and crème fraîche. Cook for another minute until well amalgamated and serve immediately.

linguine con mazzancolle
prawn & coriander
stir fry noodles

Sweet basil is native to Iran and India while coriander originates from southern Europe. Yet Italians swear by the former and Indians by the latter. Ancient Romans loved coriander, Germans flavour sausages with it, while Greeks cook pork with it. Enough of an excuse to make coriander into a pesto and try it on linguine with prawns, we thought. Hope you agree.

Serves 4
Preparation time 10 minutes
Cooking time 15 minutes

400g, 14oz, 1^1/$_2$ cups raw prawns, shells removed
1 clove of garlic, finely chopped
1 small red chilli, finely chopped
4 tbsp, 60ml, 2fl oz extra virgin olive oil
3 tbsp, 50g, ^{1}/$_4$ cup Dress Italian Coriander Pesto
350g, 12oz Thai style noodles or linguine
3 tsp freshly chopped coriander

Heat the extra virgin olive oil, chopped garlic and chilli in a heavy based frying pan or wok and stir fry for 2 minutes. Add the prawns and stir fry for a further 5 minutes until the prawns are cooked and have changed to a deep pink colour.

Drop the noodles or linguine into boiling salted water and cook according to the manufacturer's instructions. Drain the noodles, add to the frying pan with the prawns, stir in Dress Italian Coriander Pesto and freshly chopped coriander.

Season with salt and black pepper and serve immediately.

agro dolce di scampi saltati in padella e riso in bianco

steamed rice with sweet & sour prawns

Fasting days posed a particular culinary problem to medieval chefs. While plain white fish was the order of the day, that day came at the embarrassingly fast rate of one in every three. One strategy was to adapt meat recipes, including those with sweet & sour sauces. Today we'd say 'Chinese'! Boiled rice retains the intended spirit of the occasion.

Serves 4
Preparation time 15 minutes
Cooking time 25 minutes

250g, 9oz, 1 1/4 cups rice, steamed or boiled
400g, 14oz, 1 cup large shelled prawns
4 tbsp, 60ml, 2fl oz extra virgin olive oil
8 tbsp, 200g, 1/2 cup Dress Italian Pasticcio all'Agrodolce
salt and black pepper
1 clove of garlic, finely chopped
1 small red chilli, finely chopped
120ml, 4fl oz, 1/2 cup dry white wine
3 fresh mint leaves, finely chopped

Heat the olive oil, garlic & chilli in a frying pan and sauté for 2 minutes. Add the prawns and pour over the white wine. Allow the wine to reduce and pour over Dress Italian Pasticcio all'Agrodolce. Season with salt and pepper.

Add the mint leaves, stir and serve immediately on a bed of steamed or boiled rice.

tonno scottato al pepe nero
seared peppered tuna
with rialto dressing

Fresh tuna, particularly the *ventresca* underbelly of Mediterranean Bluefin, has a meaty flavour and texture that is lost when canned. Recipes for fresh tuna abound in Sicily, home to the *tonnara* fishing fleets. Black pepper together with the honey, red onions and vinegar of Dress Italian Rialto Dressing suggest a typical *agro dolce* sauce from this region.

Serves 4
Preparation time 10 minutes
Cooking time 6 minutes

4 fresh tuna steaks
2 tbsp, 30ml, 1fl oz extra virgin olive oil
4 tsp, 14g coarse ground black pepper
4 tbsp, 60g, 1/4 cup Dress Italian Rialto Dressing

Coat both sides of the tuna steaks with a layer of coarse ground black pepper.

Heat a non-stick frying pan and pour in the extra virgin olive oil. When the oil is very hot, sear the tuna for 1 minute on each side. Pour over Dress Italian Rialto Dressing, swirl for 30 seconds and remove from the pan.

Slice the steak into 2 cm strips and serve on a bed of fresh rocket dressed with extra virgin olive oil.

If you prefer your tuna to be less rare, cook for 2-3 minutes each side.

merluzzo al forno con pesto e pumate

roast cod fillets with pesto & roasted tomatoes

Ligurians occasionally use basil sauce to dress cod, sometimes with the addition of green beans in authentic Genovese style. The introduction of succulent cherry tomatoes slow baked in a fresh garlic dressing complements the meaty texture of the cod while hinting at the delights of the denser, more chewy sun dried tomatoes.

Serves 4
Preparation time 15 minutes
Cooking time 45 minutes

4 cod fillets (or any other firm white fish) of approx 110g/4oz each in weight
250g, 9 oz, 1^1/$_2$ cups cherry tomatoes cut in half
2 cloves of garlic finely chopped
4 tbsp, 60ml, 2fl oz extra virgin olive oil
salt and black pepper
4 tbsp, 50g, ^{1}/$_4$ cup Dress Italian Basil Pesto

Preheat the oven to 220 C, 425 F, Gas mark 7

Place the halved cherry tomatoes on a baking tray and season with salt, pepper, chopped garlic and drizzle with 2 tbsp of extra virgin olive oil. Bake for at least 30 minutes until soft and slightly blackened.

Place the cod fillets in another baking dish and season with salt and black pepper. Drizzle with the remaining extra virgin olive oil and bake for 12 minutes.

Serve the fish with the roasted tomatoes and a spoonful of Dress Italian Basil Pesto.

Coda:
The roasted cherry tomatoes are also good served with grilled fish or lamb chops.

insalata calda di gamberi e zucchine

warm salad of prawns & courgettes

A contemporary restaurant classic that does not have to wear its 'Italianness' on its carefully laundered starched white sleeve. An overriding concern for fresh ingredients simply combined with effortless style is the order of the day, every day.

Serves 4
Preparation time 30 minutes
Cooking time 20 minutes

450g, 1lb, 2 cups large, shelled prawns
8 tbsp, 140g, $1/2$ cup Dress Italian Vegetable Mostarda Marinade
2 cloves of garlic, 1 whole, 1 chopped finely
1 small red chilli, finely chopped
4 tbsp, 60ml, 2fl oz extra virgin olive oil
3 courgettes, sliced lengthways into long batons
juice of 1 lemon
salt and black pepper
6 fresh mint leaves

Marinate the prawns in Dress Italian Vegetable Mostarda Marinade for at least 30 minutes.

Meanwhile, heat 2 tbsp of extra virgin olive oil in a pan with the chopped chilli and a whole clove of garlic. Sauté for two minutes before adding the courgettes. Season with salt and pepper and continue to sauté for 12 minutes or until the courgettes are cooked.

Heat 2 tbsp of extra virgin olive oil in another pan with the chopped garlic. Add the marinated prawns and sauté, stirring continuously, for approximately 6 minutes.

Divide the courgettes between four plates. Top with the prawns and sprinkle with freshly chopped mint. Squeeze over the fresh lemon juice and drizzle over the remaining extra virgin olive oil.

Serve also as a starter with a chilled Pinot Grigio.

dressings

'Boil' is an ugly word. Depending on which way you look at it, *Trattoria 'Da Dora'* in Naples either serves up a magisterial *piatto unico* of vermicelli pasta cooked al dente and dressed with tomato sauce and half a whole lobster, or alternatively, half a boiled lobster, which obliges by turning red during boiling, is placed on a 'bed' of pasta dressed in a sumptuous tomato sauce, of a type that only Neapolitans can produce.

Both the pasta and the lobster have been boiled, yet the pasta is the intended beneficiary of the dressing, leaving the lobster to bathe in its reflected glory. If this is true for fish, then it is equally true for meat and vegetables; the dressings served with boiled ingredients attract little attention from food writers looking for uniquely Italian tastes and flavours.

Which is a shame, because the culinary history of Italy written into the regionally diverse combination and contrast of flavours that they encompass, suggests uses that transcend the dictates of tradition itself. To the uninitiated, these concoctions suggest a culinary safari into the dense and unmapped underbelly of a food culture that appears to offer nothing but the safe delights of standard Italian fare.

In truth, much of what is surprising, sometimes disconcerting and novel is easily brought into focus by just a smattering of knowledge about Italian food before the advent of the tomato.

spigola con mele e finocchio

seabass with fennel & apples

Seabass translates as either *Spigola* or *Branzino* on an Italian menu, depending on how it is prepared. Here the combination of wild fennel and apples subtly suggests the more overtly sweet & sour combination of oranges and wild fennel that is so typical of Moorish inspired Sicilian food. The crunchiness of the sliced apples gives added texture.

Serves 4
Preparation time 15 minutes
Cooking time 20 minutes

4 seabass fillets, boned and skinned
2 red apples cut into quarters, unpeeled
2 fennel bulbs sliced into 1 cm thick pieces
6 tbsp, 90ml, 3fl oz extra virgin olive oil
4 tbsp, 60g, 1/4 cup Dress Italian Ballaro' Dressing
salt and black pepper
1 small red chilli finely chopped

Heat 3 tbsp of extra virgin olive oil in a frying pan and sauté the apples and fennel until lightly browned but still slightly crunchy. Remove from the pan with a slotted spoon.

Season the seabass with salt and black pepper and sauté in the extra virgin olive oil and apple juices for about 4 minutes each side or until cooked through. Remove and keep warm.

Pour Dress Italian Ballaro' Dressing into the warm pan and heat gently for 20 seconds.

Divide the cooked apples and fennel between four plates. Lay a seabass fillet on each and drizzle with the warmed Dress Italian Ballaro' dressing.

filetti di salmone marinati con verdure e puré di patate
salmon with spring onion mash

This recipe works well with swordfish, fresh tuna and especially salmon with which the mustard base vegetable marinade has probably the greatest affinity. However distinctively Italian the combination of capers and anchovies, it is salmon's ability to encompass such a diverse range of complex flavours that is showcased.

Serves 4
Preparation time 40 minutes
Cooking time 30 minutes

4 salmon cutlets or steaks
8 tbsp, 140g, $1/2$ cup Dress Italian Vegetable Mostarda Marinade
2 tbsp, 30ml, 1fl oz extra virgin olive oil
salt and black pepper

for the mash
500g, 1lb, 3 cups potatoes
50g, 2oz, 4 tbsp, $1/8$ cup unsalted butter
2 tbsp, 30ml, 1fl oz extra virgin olive oil
2 small spring onions finely chopped
6 fresh mint leaves, finely chopped
salt and black pepper

Marinate the salmon steaks in Dress Italian Vegetable Mostarda for at least 30 minutes.

Meanwhile, cook the potatoes in boiling salted water until tender. Drain, peel and mash until very smooth. Stir in the butter and extra virgin olive oil with a wooden spoon while still hot. Season with salt and pepper, add the chopped spring onions and mint, stir well, set aside and keep warm.

Remove the salmon steaks from the marinade and season with salt and pepper. Heat the extra virgin olive oil in a non-stick pan and cook the salmon fillets for 2 minutes on each side (more if you like your salmon well done).

Serve immediately on a the bed of piping hot mashed potatoes.

crocchette di granchio patate e coriandolo

crab, coriander & potato cakes

Eat English, think Italian. While eating our favourite fish cakes at Joe's Cafe in Chelsea, we strayed into a discussion on *Canederli*, fried bread- crumbed gnocchi from Friuli and whether they could be made with coriander, rather than just speck, mushrooms, cheese or parsley.
Undoubtedly: but we decided to customise fish cakes instead.

Serves 4

Preparation time 30 minutes
Cooking time 10 minutes

500g , 1lb 2oz, 3 cups potatoes boiled and mashed
340g, 12oz, 1 cup flaked cooked or tinned crab or 2 large dressed crabs, brown and white meat
3 tbsp, 50g, ¼ cup Dress Italian Thai Coriander Pesto
1 small red chilli finely chopped
3 large eggs
salt and black pepper
zest of 1 lemon finely grated
200g fresh breadcrumbs
1 tbsp extra virgin olive oil
100g plain flour

for the dipping sauce:
2 tbsp mayonnaise
1 tbsp Dress Italian Thai Coriander Pesto
1 tbsp crème fraîche

Preheat the oven to 220 C, 450 F, Gas mark 7

Mix the mashed potatoes with the crab, 1 egg, the chilli, Dress Italian Coriander Pesto and the zest of one lemon. Mould the mixture into 8 patties. Beat the remaining 2 eggs. Dust the patties with flour and dip each patty into the beaten eggs. Cover each patty with breadcrumbs, ensuring that they are fully coated.

Meanwhile, mix together all the ingredients for the dipping sauce and set aside. Place the crab cakes on a baking tray, drizzle with extra virgin olive oil and bake for 10 minutes. Remove from the oven, pat dry with kitchen paper and serve with the dipping sauce.

baccalà già bagnato al pomodoro

roast cod with lemon rind & fresh tomato sauce

Soaked salt cod, or *baccalà*, displayed in shallow stainless steel sinks with constant running water to wash away the salt preservative is a common feature of fish markets throughout Italy. The Campania region offers this simplest of recipes. Fresh tomato sauce can serve as either an accompaniment as here, or as a sauce when baking.

Serves 4
Preparation time 10 minutes
Cooking time 10 minutes

4 x 250g cod fillets
grated rind of 2 lemons
4 tbsp, 60ml, 2fl oz extra virgin olive oil
salt and black pepper
10 tbsp, 1 cup Dress Italian Salsa Madre

Heat the olive oil and the lemon rind together in a non-stick pan. When hot, pan fry the cod fillets for 4 minutes on each side. Season with salt and pepper.

Gently heat Dress Italian Salsa Madre in another pan for 1 minute.

Serve each cod fillet with a spoonful of warm Dress Italian Salsa Madre and a fresh rocket salad.

tartare di salmone all'agro
tartare of salmon, spring onions & mint

Raw salmon, chopped and diced, together with finely minced onions is marinated in a typically Sicilian preparation of lemon juice, orange peel and extra virgin olive oil. To this *Agro* are added chilli and mint to enhance the contrast between the citrus flavours and the mild sourness of the onions that stops short of a full blown *agro dolce*.

Serves 4
Preparation time 20 minutes
Standing time 25 minutes

4 salmon fillets, skinned and boned
4 tbsp, 60g, ¼ cup Dress Italian Ballaro' Dressing
2 spring onions, finely chopped
juice of 2 lemons
salt and black pepper
8 fresh mint leaves chopped
1 small red chilli finely chopped
rind of ½ orange, sliced julienne or very finely
3 tbsp, 45ml, 1½ fl oz extra virgin olive oil

Chop and dice the salmon into 2cm cubes. Mix together the spring onions with the lemon juice, chilli, mint leaves and orange rind in a bowl, gradually adding the extra virgin olive oil to achieve an emulsion. Season with salt and pepper. Stir in Dress Italian Ballaro' Dressing.

Add the salmon and mix well.

Cover the bowl and refrigerate for 25 minutes and serve with a fresh green salad.

Coda:
This dish cannot be stored and has to be prepared and eaten immediately. Use a very small bird's eye chilli. If you don't want the flavour too spicy, remove the seeds.

carré d'agnello in cartoccio
rack of lamb with garlic & rosemary

Today's tradition is yesterday's innovation. Why balsamic vinegar replaced the original lemon & sugar or honey agro dolce that may also have served as a preparatory marinade is long forgotten. Here, honey is re-introduced, while oven baking the meat *in cartoccio* rather than as a casserole helps keep the meat moist without the need to add water.

Serves 4
Preparation time 12 minutes
Cooking time 35 minutes

1 rack of lamb (with 8 cutlets)
4 sprigs of fresh rosemary
4 tsp, 50g, 1/4 cup Dress Italian Balsamic Honey Glaze
salt and freshly ground black pepper
4 tbsp, 60ml, 2 fl oz extra virgin olive oil
4 cloves of garlic sliced in half

for the crunchy baked potatoes
4 large potatoes, peeled and quartered
4 cloves of garlic
a few sprigs of rosemary
3 tbsp extra virgin olive oil
salt

Preheat oven to 220 C, 425 F, Gas mark 7

Place the lamb on a baking tray. Season with salt and pepper. Place the garlic cloves and rosemary sprigs in the fold of the meat near the bone. Drizzle with the extra virgin olive oil. Brush over with Dress Italian Balsamic Honey Glaze, cover the lamb with aluminium foil and bake in the preheated oven for 35 minutes.

Meanwhile, boil the potatoes for 10 minutes and drain. Sprinkle with salt and place on a baking tray. Scatter over the rosemary sprigs and the 4 garlic cloves and drizzle with extra virgin olive oil. Bake in the oven for 30 minutes or until golden brown.

Baste the lamb every 10 minutes or so with the pan juices. Remove the foil for the final 3 minutes of baking to give the meat a golden colour.

Remove the lamb from the baking tray and divide into cutlets. Serve two cutlets per person drizzled with the juice from the pan and the crisp roast potatoes.

braciola di maiale
pork cutlets with l'orientale mash

Pork is used so extensively in the preparation of Italian food - for cured meats, or as an ingredient for pasta fillings, sauces and cooking sausages - that more obvious dishes such as *arista, porchetta & maiale al latte* are often overlooked. So here is a simple reminder. The tart sweetness of the mashed potato counterbalances the fattiness of the pork.

Serves 4
Preparation time 15 minutes
Cooking time 30 minutes

4 pork cutlets (approx 150g, 5 oz each)
3 tbsp, 45ml, 1 1/2fl oz extra virgin olive oil
salt and black pepper
1 tsp fresh thyme

For the mash
500g, 1lb, 3 cups potatoes
4 tbsp, 50g, 1/3 cup salted butter
4 tbsp, 60g, 1/4 cup Dress Italian L'Orientale Dressing
4 tbsp, 1fl oz, 1/8 cup double cream
salt and freshly ground black pepper
A few toasted pine nuts

Boil the potatoes in their skins for 20 minutes or until soft. Meanwhile, season the pork chops with salt and pepper. Heat the extra virgin olive oil in a frying pan and when the oil is hot, cook the pork chops for about 5 minutes on each side. Sprinkle chopped fresh thyme over the pork.

Drain the potatoes and peel and mash while still hot. Mix the mashed potato with Dress Italian L'Orientale Dressing, butter and cream and stir with a wooden spoon until all the ingredients are combined. Season to taste.

Serve the pork on a bed of mashed potato drizzled with the pan juices and a sprinkling of pine nuts.

Coda:
For a really creamy mash use red skinned or waxy potatoes. Boiling potatoes in their skins prevents them from absorbing excess water making a lovely fluffy light mash

anatra alla frutta
marinated duck breast with pears

The Venetian mainland has many versions of this classic dish. Traditionally, pears would have served as a stuffing for the whole duck cooked in an earthenware pot. While some recipes suggest the further addition of grappa made from pears, what instead could be better than using locally produced mostarda di pere.

Serves 4
Preparation time 30 minutes
Cooking time 20 minutes

4 skinned duck breasts
4 pears, peeled and quartered
8 tbsp, 140g, 1/2 cup Dress Italian Pear Mostarda Marinade
salt and black pepper
2 tbsp, 30ml, 1fl oz extra virgin olive oil

Place the duck breasts in a bowl and cover with 6 tbsp of Dress Italian Pear Mostarda Marinade. Marinate the pears with the remaining marinade in another bowl. Cover and place in the refrigerator to marinate for at least 30 minutes.

Heat the extra virgin olive oil in a non-stick frying pan. Add the duck breasts and cook for 6 minutes on each side stirring occasionally to prevent the duck from sticking. In another pan, cook the marinated pears in 8 tbsp of water for about 15 minutes.

Season the duck breasts with salt and pepper and serve with pears. Accompany with freshly steamed green vegetables or a sautéed curly kale.

brasato di stinco d'agnello al vino rosso

braised lamb shanks with red wine

Be prepared to sacrifice one bottle of red wine for a good cause! As the name *brasato di manzo al Barolo* suggests, the Piedmontese are prepared to go that extra kilometre, but an inexpensive Cabernet Sauvignon will do just as well. The red wine acts as a base for the marinade to which other ingredients are added. Heady stuff!

Serves 4
Preparation time 20 minutes
Cooking time 1^1/$_2$ hours

4 x 350g lamb shanks
600g, 1^1/$_2$lb, 4 cups root vegetables (parsnips, turnips, leeks)
400g, 14oz, 2^1/$_2$ cups carrots peeled & cut into pieces
4 tbsp, 50g, ^{1}/$_4$ cup Dress Italian Ginger & Parsley Pesto
500ml, 16fl oz, 2 cups red wine
6 tbsp, 90ml, 3fl oz extra virgin olive oil
salt and black pepper

Make an incision into each lamb shank and rub a teaspoon of Dress Italian Ginger & Parsley Pesto into each cut, close to the bone. Season each shank with salt and black pepper.

Heat the extra virgin olive oil in a large heavy based saucepan and sauté the vegetables for 10 minutes. Add the lamb shanks and sauté for a further 10 minutes to seal the meat on all sides. Pour over 2 cups of red wine and turn the heat down low. Slowly cook for 1 hour or until the meat is tender and beginning to come away from the bone. Add some water or stock as the liquid evaporates during cooking.

Once cooked, remove the shanks and the vegetables from the pan and reduce the remaining liquid to a sauce-like consistency.

Serve hot with mashed potatoes mixed with fresh parsley and extra virgin olive oil .

portafoglio di maiale al mascarpone

pork wrapped in pancetta with a mascarpone filling

Portafoglio, literally 'wallet', is an old fashioned culinary term that aptly describes the role of the incisions cut into raw tenderloin. The essential fats and flavours they contain keep a pork roast tender and tasty. *Mascarpone*, blended with Forcella, keeps the roast moist and forms a satisfying sauce with the natural juices of the *pancetta*.

Serves 4
Preparation time 25 minutes
Cooking time 30 minutes

2 x 350g, 12oz pork fillets
8 slices pancetta or unsmoked streaky bacon, finely sliced
10 fresh sage leaves
4 tbsp, 60ml, 2fl oz extra virgin olive oil
150 ml, 5 fl oz, 1/3 pint white wine

Filling
3 tbsp, 60g, 1/4 cup Dress Italian Forcella Dressing
4 tbsp, 100g, 1/2 cup mascarpone
salt and freshly ground black pepper

Preheat the oven to 220 C, 425 F, Gas mark 7

Mix together Dress Italian Forcella Dressing and mascarpone in a bowl and season with black pepper. Cut five incisions (3cm long and 2 cm deep) along each pork fillet to create 5 'pockets'. Fill each pocket with 2 tbsp of mascarpone blended with Dress Italian Forcella Dressing. Season the fillets with salt and pepper. Place 5 sage leaves along the top of each fillet and wrap the pancetta slices around each. Place the pork on a baking dish and drizzle with extra virgin olive oil. Bake for 25 minutes or until the pork juices run clear. After 10 minutes, pour over the white wine and continue baking for the remaining 15 minutes. Remove from the oven and slice.

Serve drizzled with the pan juices on a bed of mashed potato.

Coda:
For a thicker, creamier sauce, pour the pan juices into a small saucepan and reduce. Stir in 1 tbsp of mascarpone and serve immediately.
For mashed potato with a difference, add 2 tbsp of Dress Italian Forcella Dressing

pasticcio

In culinary terms, 'pasticcio' represents one

of the grandest Renaissance extravaganzas, a culinary masterpiece with the sumptuous breadth of a Veronese canvas and a list of ingredients to leave you breathless.

The pairing of a savoury meat *Ragù* made with beef, ham, chicken breast and livers, porcini mushrooms, carrots, celery, onions, chicken broth, together with pasta and a *besciamella* sauce, encased in a slightly sweet pastry crust, suggests both a continued fascination with the Ancient Roman and Arab traditions of sweet and sour, and a typically Italian solution to a culinary dilemma: under Sumptuary laws, when Italians were enjoined by the papacy to eat no more than 2 to 3 courses per meal, what better way of overcoming such a stricture than by combining the ingredients of several courses into one dish!

Unless you have tasted such a dish - a particularly fine version can be found at Ristorante Fini, in Modena - you would be forgiven for (initially) exclaiming: 'What a mess!', oblivious to the fact that such is the precise meaning of *Pasticcio* in everyday Italian parlance, and that the engendering of such a surprise from the recipient at the moment of impact is precisely the reaction sought.

With that in mind, it is not surprising that the term has survived on restaurant menus despite being given an increasingly loose interpretation by chefs more interested in asserting their professional individuality against the rigors of custom.

To term a dish a *Pasticcio* is to suggest that the creator is taking 'time out' from 'tradition' in order to take a few hopefully felicitous liberties and to explore new combinations with favourite ingredients. If tradition is an experiment that worked, then the creator of a *Pasticcio* is hoping to create a future classic. Who is to say that *Pesto* itself was not firstly welcomed with the exclamation of 'what a fine mess!'

It is a short distance from here to that other art of which Italians are masters: *arrangiarsi*, the ability to improvise or 'make do' with what one has to hand, be it in every day life, or while rustling something delicious up in the kitchen with what's left in the fridge.

timballo di melanzane con polpette

aubergine parcels filled with meatballs

Here's a variation on the versatile Sicilian classic of meatballs in tomato sauce. Rather than cooking meatballs in tomato sauce and serving the combination on pasta or separately as a main dish, here they are deep fried and mixed with a peperonata style sauce before being enclosed in a timballo of deep fried aubergine.

Serves 4
Preparation time 40 minutes
Cooking time 20 minutes

2 aubergines sliced lengthways (1cm thick)
2 tbsp, 30ml, 1fl oz extra virgin olive oil
8 fresh basil leaves
sunflower oil for deep frying
1 jar, 280g Dress Italian Pasticcio di Peperoni

for the meatballs
500g, 1lb, 2 cups very lean minced meat
1 egg
6 fresh mint leaves, chopped
1 small red chilli, finely chopped
1 clove of garlic, finely chopped
salt and black pepper

Preheat the oven to 220 C, 425 F, Gas mark 6.
Heat the sunflower oil in a heavy based saucepan. Dust the aubergine slices with a little flour and when the oil is very hot, deep fry the slices both sides for a few minutes until golden. Pat dry with kitchen paper. Mix the minced meat with the egg, mint, red chilli, garlic, salt and pepper. Roll into small round balls. Deep fry in the sunflower oil for 3 minutes, remove, and drain on kitchen paper to absorb any excess oil.
In a fresh saucepan, heat the extra virgin olive oil with the basil leaves and when hot add Dress Italian Pasticcio di Peperoni. Cook for 2 minutes, add the deep fried meatballs and gently simmer for 3 minutes. Line individual ramekin dishes with the aubergine slices. Make sure they overhang the dish. Fill with the meatballs and Pasticcio sauce and fold over the overhanging pieces to close the parcel. Place in the oven and bake for 10 minutes. Serve hot with fresh crusty bread.

Coda:
The meatball recipe can also be used for mini burgers, see pages 26 & 27

petto di pollo con fichi e radicchio

warm salad with chicken, figs & radicchio

Chicken or duck may be the main ingredient of this *Friuli-Venezia Giulia* inspired recipe, but the real stars are the sautéed figs and baked *radicchio* dressed in a sweet & sour dressing made with lemon juice, sugar, pine nuts & black pepper that performs the role of a traditional Venetian *Soar* without the need to firstly marinate the chicken or duck.

Serves 4
Preparation time 10 minutes
Cooking time 20 minutes

4 chicken breasts, skin removed
2 heads of radicchio cut into quarters
4 ripe figs cut in half
6 tbsp, 90ml, 3fl oz extra virgin olive oil
4 tbsp, 60g, 1/4 cup Dress Italian L'Orientale Dressing
salt and black pepper

Place the radicchio on a baking tray. Drizzle 2 tbsp of extra virgin olive oil over the radicchio quarters and place under a hot grill for approximately 5 minutes or until the leaves have softened and the radicchio turns a dark purple.

Heat 3 tbsp of extra virgin olive oil in a frying pan and when hot sauté the chicken breasts for 5 minutes on each side or until cooked through. Season with salt and black pepper. Meanwhile, sauté the figs with the remaining tablespoon of extra virgin olive oil for one minute. Remove the figs from the pan and add Dress Italian L'Orientale Dressing to warm through for 20 seconds.

Place 2 pieces of radicchio on each plate, followed by the chicken and top with the cooked figs.

Pour over the warmed Dress Italian L'Orientale Dressing and serve.

lombo di maiale con peperoni in agrodolce

pork cutlets with sweet & sour sauce

In the Middle Ages pork loin was cooked in a sweet & sour sauce containing white wine, vinegar and ginger, thickened with dates, currants and pine nuts to provide the 'sweet' contrast that pre-dates the Arabic introduction of almonds as a thickener & lemon juice as a replacement for vinegar - it was left to the Italians to think of combining it with pork.

Serves 4
Preparation time 5 minutes
Cooking time 15 minutes

4 pork cutlets
salt and black pepper
sprig of fresh rosemary
2 tbsp, 30ml, 1fl oz extra virgin olive oil
7 tbsp, 200g, 3/4 cup Dress Italian Pasticcio all'Agrodolce

In a non-stick frying pan, heat the extra virgin olive oil with the rosemary and when hot, cook the pork cutlets on each side for about 6 minutes. Season with salt and pepper and remove.

Warm Dress Italian Pasticcio all'Agrodolce with the pan juices for one minute and serve next to the cutlets.

tagine farsu alla siciliana
baked chicken with apricots, prunes & couscous

The emblematic *Cuscusso alla Trapanese* from south east Sicily bears eloquent testimony to the continuing affinity between Sicilian and north African food with their shared tradition for combining vegetables and fruit with sour ingredients. This dish combines elements of Sicilian and Moroccan food, hopefully in equal measure.

Serves 4
Preparation time 30 minutes
Cooking time 1 1/2 hours

1 large free range chicken approx. 1.7kg
4 red onions peeled and cut into quarters
6 carrots peeled and cut into large pieces
6 tbsp, 90ml, 2fl oz extra virgin olive oil
14 ready to eat dried apricots
14 pitted prunes
4 tbsp, 50g, 2oz, 1/4 cup sultanas or golden raisins
3 tbsp, 50g, 1/4 cup Dress Italian Ginger & Parsley Pesto
480ml, 116 fl oz, 2 cups dry white wine
salt and black pepper
2 small red chillis finely chopped
2 lemons cut into quarters
juice of 1 lemon

for the Couscous
250g, 9 oz couscous
4 finely chopped spring onions
fresh mint leaves
salt and black pepper
4 tbsp, 50g, 1/4 cup softened butter or extra virgin olive oil

Preheat the oven to 220 C, 425 F, Gas mark 6

Rub the skin of the chicken with salt and pepper. Gently separate the skin from the flesh at the neck and carefully rub 2 tbsp of Dress Italian Ginger and Parsley Pesto directly onto the breast meat. Stuff the chicken with the remaining Dress Italian Ginger and Parsley Pesto, 4 pieces of lemon, 4 slices of onion and 8 each of the apricots and prunes.

Meanwhile, place the remaining onion and carrots in a roasting dish, drizzle with 3 tbsp of the extra virgin olive oil and season with salt and pepper. Place the chicken on top and scatter over the remaining lemon quarters. Pour the lemon juice and the remaining extra virgin olive oil over the chicken. Cover with aluminium foil and place in the oven.

After 25 minutes, remove the foil and pour over a glass of wine. Cover and return to the oven to cook for a further 25 minutes.

Pour over the remaining wine and scatter the remaining dried fruit around the chicken and continue baking uncovered for a further 20 minutes or until the chicken is golden brown and the juices around the thighs run clear when pricked with a skewer.

Cook the couscous according to the manufacturer's instructions. Dress the couscous with the spring onions and mint and season with salt and black pepper. Stir in the butter or extra virgin olive oil. Spoon the couscous onto a large serving dish, place the cooked chicken in the centre and dress with the vegetables and fruit. Pour over the pan juices and serve.

Coda:
This dish also works well with poussin, serve one per person.

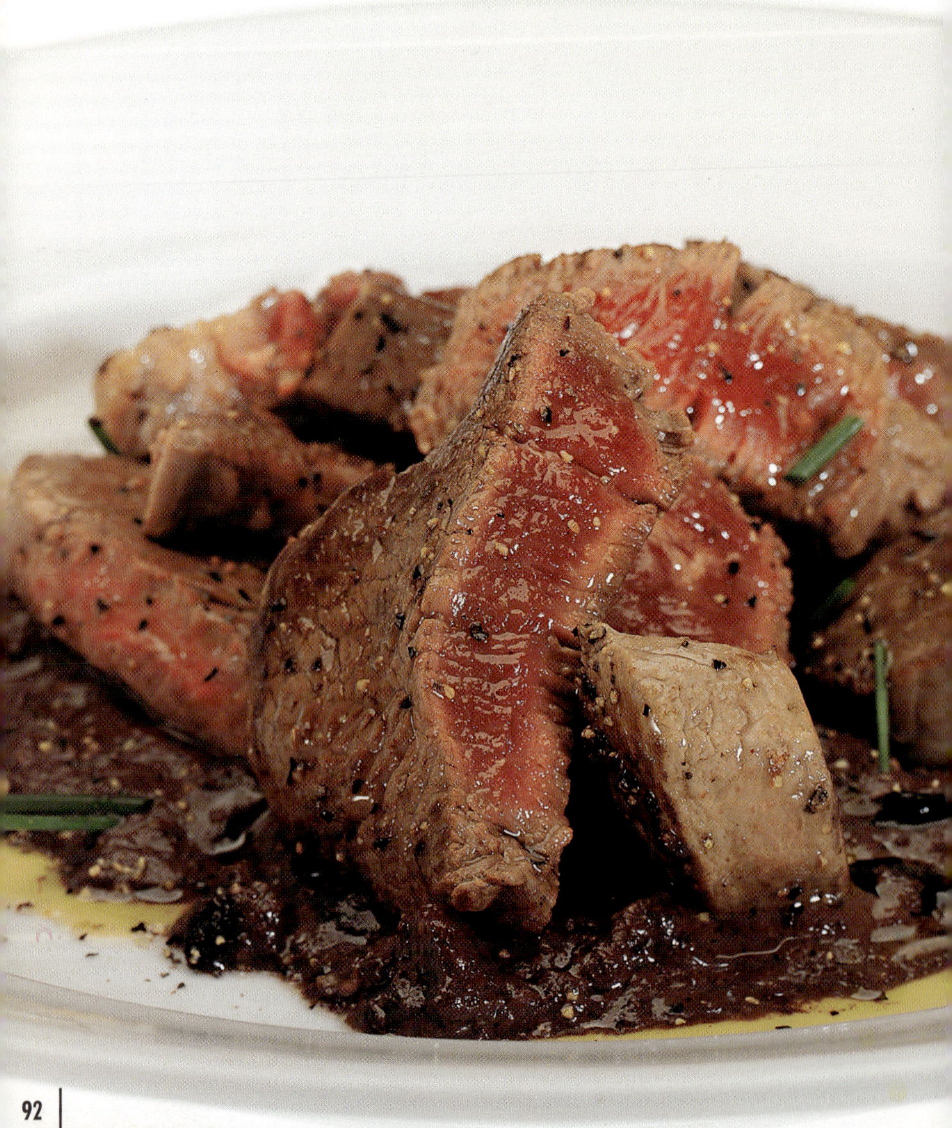

tagliata di manzo
beef fillet with black olives

Very Tuscan and very simple. Tuscans themselves also use the locally reared & renowned pure Chianina strain of beef for the monumental *Bistecca alla Fiorentina*. Dress Italian Forcella Dressing, olive paste and fresh chives provide a successful alternative to the traditional accompaniment of sautéed fresh porcini mushrooms.

Serves 4
Preparation time 10 minutes
Cooking time 10 minutes

4 beef fillet steaks approx 200g, 7oz each
3 tbsp, 45ml, 1 1/2 fl oz extra virgin olive oil
salt and freshly ground black pepper
3 tbsp, 60g, 1/4 cup Dress Italian Forcella Dressing
1 tbsp, 20g black olive paste
salt and pepper to taste
chopped fresh chives

Season each fillet with salt and pepper. Heat the extra virgin olive oil in a frying pan and cook the fillets for 5 minutes on each side or to preference.

Combine the olive paste and Dress Italian Forcella Dressing.

Remove the fillets from the pan. Swirl Dress Italian Forcella Dressing and olive paste in the hot pan until warmed through (approximately 20 seconds).

Place a spoon of the warmed Dress Italian Forcella Dressing on each plate. Slice the cooked fillet and place on top. Sprinkle with finely chopped chives and a drizzle of extra virgin olive oil and serve immediately with a fresh rocket salad.

Coda:
Cut the raw fillet into chunky slices and stir fry. Serve with mashed potatoes mixed with 1 tbsp of Dress Italian Forcella Dressing.

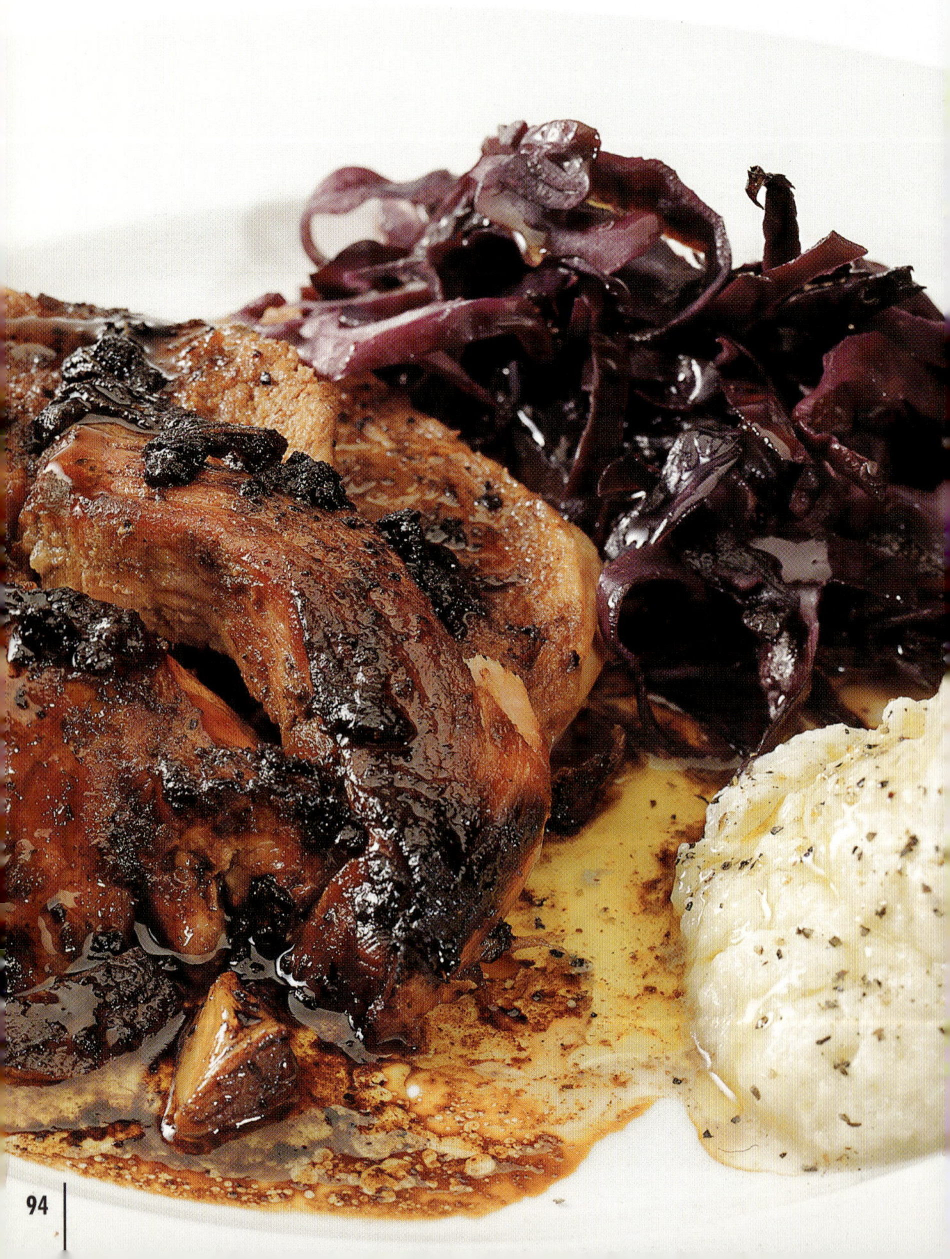

capriolo marinato alle pere con verza rossa

marinated venison with red cabbage

You can 'suffocate' red cabbage into submission Venetian style by cooking it very slowly with a small amount of liquid in a covered pan - a method called *sofegao*. Red cabbage is also used to great effect with game sweetened with pears, here achieved by sautéing them in Dress Italian Pear Mostarda Marinade used for tenderising the venison.

Serves 4
Preparation time 40 minutes
Cooking time 30 minutes

4 x 250g venison steaks
8tbsp, 140g, $^1/_2$ cup Dress Italian Pear Mostarda Marinade
salt and black pepper
300g, 120 oz, 3 cups red cabbage cut finely
450g, 1lb parsnips peeled and boiled
4 tbsp, 60 ml, 2fl oz extra virgin olive oil
3 tbsp salted butter
a fresh bay leaf

Place the venison fillets in a shallow dish and cover with Dress Italian Pear Marinade. Leave to marinate for at least 30 minutes. Meanwhile, boil the parsnips in salted water until tender.

Blanch the red cabbage in boiling salted water for 3 minutes, drain and run under cold water. Pat dry with kitchen paper. In a non-stick pan, heat 2 tbsp of the extra virgin olive oil, add the bay leaf and the red cabbage. Season with salt and black pepper and sauté for 6 minutes. Remove from the heat.

Drain the boiled parsnips and mash well. Stir in the butter, salt and black pepper until smooth.

In another non-stick pan, add 2 tbsp of extra virgin olive oil and pan fry the venison for approximately 7 minutes on each side or to taste. Season with salt and black pepper.

Drizzle pan juices over the venison before serving with the parsnip mash and cabbage.

mostarde

A veritable north Italian icon, given lip service but rarely savoured, this relic of the eighteenth century table sits, in a blush of colour, stranded on modern day food shelves, a specimen from the past, collecting dust.

Like the life sized terracotta image of some locally revered patron saint, honoured only through the hardened arteries of ritual, Mostarda is now given an outing only at Christmas time, served as an accompaniment with bollito, unless used by diehard traditionalists as seemingly out of touch with the modern world as the condiment itself.

Has mostarda therefore reached the end of its evolutionary cycle, destined to disappear along with such food history book teasers as Lodigiano cheese and Ruta? We think not. But leave it to the Italians who can mistake evolution with iconoclasm and it just might. It is ironic that we, with our familiarity with relishes and Indian food, are probably better equipped to see the blindingly obvious.

A brief historical refresher will hopefully convince you.

Mustard or 'senape' - not to be confused with 'mostarda' - based mixtures including olive oil, vinegar or wine must, honey and herbs served as a marinade for both meats and fish, especially tuna, and as a condiment to be served with anything from boiled meats, fish, vegetables and wild boar. By the fourteenth century, the first modern interpretation of mostarda - a mustard based whole or sliced fruit preserve served as a side relish - began to emerge alongside its existing uses as a marinade or condiment, and at a time when sugar superseded honey as a sweetener throughout Europe.

By the eighteenth century, we begin to have written confirmation of what are recognisably 'mostarde' as understood by Italians today. Methods may have changed, but the product has remained essentially the same since, gradually losing its role as a marinade and preservative, barely surviving as a condiment, with the few exceptions such as Piedmontese salsa d'api. Cut off from other ingredients, either as an accompaniment almost exclusively for boiled meats, and occasionally mascarpone cheese, its days in the kitchen were long past, other than its oft-mentioned role as part of the ingredients for the pumpkin stuffing of Ravioli, Mantova style.

Time to put Mostarda back on the culinary map by recreating its role as the principle ingredient in a range of regionally inspired marinades of which we hope these will be just the beginning.

quaglie in cartoccio con riso
roasted quail on a bed of saffron risotto

The image of quails being shot in season while flying across the Venetian lagoon will have little relevance to the farm-reared variety you find in stores. More importantly they are small enough to be marinated whole which in turn provides an elegant dish when served on a bed of saffron flavoured rice, as Lombardy tradition dictates.

Serves 4
Preparation time 40 minutes
Cooking time 30 minutes

4 quails, cleaned
4 tbsp, 60ml, 2fl oz extra virgin olive oil
salt and black pepper
8 fresh sage leaves
8tbsp, 140g, $1/2$ cup Dress Italian Clementine Mostarda Marinade

for the risotto
350g, 12oz, $1^1/2$ cups American 'Easy Cook' long grain white rice
50g, 2oz, $1/4$ cup unsalted butter
3 saffron threads, 0.125g saffron
50g, 2oz, $1/8$ cup Parmigiano Reggiano freshly grated
salt and black pepper
2 tbsp single cream

Preheat oven to 220 C, 425 F, Gas mark 7

Marinate the quails in Dress Italian Clementine Mostarda Marinade for at least 30 minutes.

Place the quails on a baking tray and dress with extra virgin olive oil and season with salt and pepper. Dress with sage leaves, cover with foil and bake in the oven for about 30 minutes. Remove the foil after 20 minutes and bake uncovered for the remaining 10 minutes.

Meanwhile, gently simmer the butter and cream and stir in the saffron. Remove from the heat. Boil the rice for about 12 minutes and when al dente drain and toss with the saffron sauce adding salt, black pepper and Parmigiano Reggiano.

Stir well and place one whole quail on a bed of risotto to serve.

pollo marinato con cavolo nero

marinated chicken with black cabbage

Food market stalls throughout Tuscany creak under the weight of Cavolo Nero as autumn turns to winter and thoughts turn to thick vegetable and broadbean soups such as the renowned ribollita. Nearer home, Cavolo Nero provides much needed moisture when braising chicken, whilst releasing its natural sweetness.

Serves 4
Preparation time 35 minutes
Cooking time 30 minutes

4 skinned chicken breasts
8 tbsp, 140g, 1/2 cup Dress Italian Vegetable Mostarda Marinade
salt and black pepper
4 tbsp, 60ml, 2fl oz extra virgin olive oil
450g, 1lb black cabbage, roughly chopped
200g cherry tomatoes on the vine

Preheat the oven to 220 C, 425 F, Gas Mark 7

Make 3 incisions in the chicken breast and marinate the chicken for at least 30 minutes with Dress Italian Vegetable Mostarda Marinade.

Blanch the black cabbage in boiling water for 4 minutes and drain. Toss with 2 tbsp of extra virgin olive oil and season with black pepper. Allow to cool to room temperature. Place the cherry tomatoes on an oven tray, drizzle with extra virgin olive oil and bake for 15 minutes.

Heat the remaining extra virgin olive oil in a non-stick pan. Pan fry the marinated chicken breasts for about 8 minutes on each side or until thoroughly cooked. Season with salt and black pepper.

Serve the chicken drizzled with the pan juices and a side helping of dressed black cabbage and baked tomatoes.

Coda:
If black cabbage is unavailable, try serving the chicken with blanched mange tout instead.

prosciutto al forno con pere ubriache

baked gammon & pears in red wine

Inspiration comes from pears poached in red wine, a tradition that Friuli-Venezia Giulia shares with Piedmont. Forsake the locally produced thickly cut slices of otherwise delicious San Daniele cured ham for gammon steaks marinated in Dress Italian Pear Mostarda Marinade for extra flavour. James Joyce, who lived for a time in Trieste, Friuli's capital city, would have undoubtedly approved.

Serves 4
Preparation time 25 minutes
Cooking time 1 hour 10 minutes

450g/1lb gammon
2tbsp, 30ml, 1fl oz extra virgin olive oil
salt and black pepper
4 firm pears, peeled
600ml, 20fl oz, 1 pint red wine
$1/3$ tsp ground cinnamon
1 fresh bay leaf
8tbsp, 140g, $1/2$ cup Dress Italian Pear Mostarda Marinade
1 tbsp castor sugar
5 sprigs of rosemary

Preheat the oven to 220 C, 425 F, Gas mark 7

Marinate the gammon in Dress Italian Pear Mostarda Marinade for at least 30 minutes. Meanwhile, pour the red wine into a saucepan and add the pears. Add the bay leaf, cinnamon and sugar and simmer gently for 40 minutes or until the red wine has been reduced to a syrupy consistency.

Place the gammon on a greased baking tray on top of the sprigs of rosemary. Drizzle with the extra virgin olive oil and season with salt and black pepper. Cover with aluminium foil and bake for 50 minutes. Remove the foil and continue baking for a further 10 minutes. Remove from the oven and slice.

Take the pears out of the red wine sauce with a slotted spoon and slice. Divide the pear slices between 4 plates and top with the gammon. Drizzle with red wine sauce and a pinch of cinnamon and serve.

spiedini di manzo e peperoni
barbecued, skewered beef

I wouldn't think of ordering what is essentially a kebab when 'eating out', other than in my own back garden. While restaurant chefs deserve greater challenges, more imaginative marinades nevertheless promote greater confidence in falling back on proven time savers when time is in short supply.

Serves 4
Preparation time 30 minutes
Cooking time 10 minutes

400g, 14 oz, 2 cups of beef cut into large cubes
2 yellow peppers cut into large chunks
2 red peppers cut into large chunks
8 fresh bay leaves
8 tbsp, 140g, 1/2 cup Dress Italian Clementine Mostarda Marinade
salt and black peppers
4 skewers
3 tbsp extra virgin olive oil

Prepare the barbecue or heat the grill while soaking the skewers in cold water to prevent them from burning.

Mix the beef cubes with the peppers and bay leaves in a large bowl and cover with Dress Italian Clementine Mostarda Marinade for at least 30 minutes.

Thread the beef onto the skewers, followed by a chunk of red pepper, a chunk of yellow pepper and then another cube of beef. Repeat as necessary. Place a bay leaf at each end of the skewer. Brush the extra virgin olive oil over the skewers and grill or barbecue, turning regularly for 10 minutes.

Season with salt and pepper and serve immediately with a fresh, crisp, mixed leaf salad.

anatra in padella con mille verdure

stir fry of duck breast and bok choy

The Chinese quarter in Milan is Via Paolo Sarpi, which is where Susanna often meets her cousin Carlotta for lunch and a conspiratorial chinwag. Last time lunch consisted of rather less than Choyce Bok, so maybe this recipe should really be in Italian. Chat concerned Carlotta's brother Giovanni's new book. Title? 'African Soup'! *

Serves 4
Preparation time 15 minutes
Cooking time 12 - 15 minutes

2 large duck breasts, skinned and cut into slices
2 red peppers, cut finely
1 red onion, sliced finely
150g, 5 oz, 1 cup bok choy or other Asian greens, chopped
70g, 3^1/2 oz, 1 cup fresh bean sprouts
4 tbsp, 60ml, 2fl oz extra virgin olive oil
3 tbsp, 60g, ^{1}/4 cup Dress Italian Rialto Dressing
salt and freshly ground black pepper

Heat 2 tbsp of extra virgin olive oil in a wok and when hot add all the vegetables. Stir fry for 2 minutes.

Add the sliced duck breast and continue to stir fry for another 6-8 minutes. Season with salt and black pepper and add Dress Italian Rialto Dressing. Stir well and remove from the heat. Drizzle over the remaining oil and serve on a bed of egg noodles.

* Family joke. It's actually called 'African Soap' by Giovanni Mastrangelo published by Marsilio Editore, soon to be translated into English.

cipolline con miele al balsamico

caramelised baby onions

Most recipes employ balsamic vinegar enhanced with sugar to caramelise, colour and flavour baby onions, sometimes instead opting for the use of flour as a thickener. Not only can honey flavoured with a few drops of well-aged balsamic achieve better results, as hopefully this recipe proves, it also acts as a ready to use and versatile reduction as well.

Serves 4
Preparation time 10 minutes
Cooking time 25 minutes

500g, 1lb, 3 cups baby onions, peeled
6 tbsp, 90ml, 3 fl oz extra virgin olive oil
2 tbsp Dress Italian Balsamic Honey Glaze
salt and freshly ground black pepper
2 bay leaves
3 tbsp sultanas or golden raisins

Preheat the oven to 200 C, 400 F, Gas mark 6

Cook the onions in boiling salted water for 7 minutes. Drain and pat dry with kitchen paper. Place the onions on a baking tray and pour over the extra virgin olive oil. Season with salt and black pepper. Mix in the bay leaves and sultanas.

Bake in a preheated oven for 10 minutes. Drizzle the onions with Dress Italian Balsamic Honey Glaze. Bake for a further 5 minutes until the honey caramelises without burning.

Serve as a side dish to roast meats.

peperoni imbottiti di verdure
stuffed baked peppers

Most regions of Italy have recipes for stuffed baked peppers, combining a medley of ingredients including rice, breadcrumbs, tuna and anchovies. For something more *morbido*, we can combine rich Sicilian style vegetable relishes with mascarpone, ricotta or, as in this case, crème fraîche.

Serves 4
Preparation time 10 minutes
Cooking time 30 minutes

4 large red peppers
4 tbsp/60 ml/2 fl oz extra virgin olive oil

for the filling
1 jar, 280g Dress Italian Pasticcio di Verdure
1 large egg
100g, 4 oz, 2/3 cup Parmigiano Reggiano, freshly grated
1 small red chilli, freshly grated
2 tbsp crème fraîche
salt and black pepper
8 fresh basil leaves, finely chopped
4 fresh mint leaves, finely chopped
4 tbsp, 60 ml, 2 fl oz extra virgin olive oil
4 tbsp, 35g, 1/2 cup coarse toasted bread crumbs

Preheat the oven to 220 C, 425 F, Gas mark 7.

Remove the top of each pepper and scoop out the membranes and seeds.

Mix together the egg, Parmigiano Reggiano, crème fraîche, Dress Italian Pasticcio di Verdure, salt, black pepper, red chilli, basil and mint.

Fill each of the peppers with the mixture. Place on a baking tray and drizzle with the extra virgin olive oil. Bake in a preheated oven for 30 minutes. Leave to cool for at least 10 minutes and serve with a rocket salad.

Coda:
For a low fat option, replace the crème fraîche with Quark.

insalata di pere gorgonzola e pinoli

gorgonzola, pear and pine nut salad

Italian salads, other than ordinary green leaf or mixed salads, can serve as either cold or hot antipasto appetizers. Caramelised pears and mountain gorgonzola together with lambs lettuce and pine nuts make for a delicious new interpretation of this Piedmontese cheese board classic.

Serves 4
Preparation time 25 minutes
Cooking time approx 20 minutes

120g, 4 ^{1}/2oz, 4 loosely packed cups lambs lettuce
2 firm pears peeled and cut into eighths
120g, 4 ^{1}/2oz, 1 cup gorgonzola cut into cubes
30g, 1oz, ^{1}/4 cup pine nuts
salt and black pepper
4 tbsp, 60g, ^{1}/4 cup Dress Italian Ballaro' Dressing
1 tsp, 10g butter
1 tbsp, 15ml, ^{1}/2fl oz extra virgin olive oil
pinch of castor sugar

Melt the butter with a pinch of sugar in a non-stick frying pan. Add the pears and sauté for 15 minutes until golden brown and slightly caramelised. Remove from the pan and allow to cool.

Place the lambs lettuce in a large bowl and toss with 1 tbsp of extra virgin olive oil and season with salt and pepper. Arrange the leaves between four plates and place 4 pear slices on top of each. Sprinkle with pine nuts and gorgonzola cheese.

Mix Dress Italian Ballaro' Dressing with the remaining extra virgin olive oil and drizzle over each plate. Season with salt and pepper. Serve immediately.

Coda:
Add a few drops of freshly squeezed lemon juice or balsamic vinegar for a more tangy dressing.

pestos

Oh! The tyranny of tradition.

Talking about 'pesto' is like referring to one of those ubiquitous brand names that define a category - like 'Hoover' or 'Biro' - with the difference that at least with these we acknowledge, albeit obliquely, the existence of other manufactured brands serving a similar purpose. Not so Pesto. There are false pretenders to Pesto's throne that need to be summarily dispatched such as *pesto trapanese* that has metamorphosed from being basil mixed with fresh tomatoes to dry tomatoes under the forlorn and futile attempt to find legitimacy as 'red pesto', a name more in keeping with the kind of ridicule contained in the very tongue in cheek 'The Futurist Cookbook' of 1932 than to serious consideration. Even walnut sauce, which itself hails from Liguria, is referred to in other terms, salsa di noci, in hushed respect to its more famous, though considerably younger rival. Yet, isn't a salsa di noci 'pesto' under any other name?

Let's leave (almost) the last word to Pellegrino Artusi, who in his 'The Science of Cookery & the Art of Eating Well' of 1891 had this to say:

> *Lenten spaghetti: Many who read this recipe will exclaim "what a ridiculous dish!" But I like it. It's from Romagna and if you serve it to young people you can be sure of their approval. Mash walnuts with breadcrumbs, add some confectioner's sugar and a pinch of spices - nutmeg, cinnamon, all spice, cloves, sweet almonds. Drain the pasta, season it with oil and pepper, stir in the PESTO and serve it.*

Like it or not, the history of 'pesto', from ancient Rome to the Renaissance - when walnuts were used as a thickener - is written in this venerable recipe. And while Artusi has been much criticised for not including what we could recognise as pesto in his book, the recipe usually cited as evidence for this grave omission instead states:

> *La buttuta o savore d'aglio: Recipe 39: Take 3 or 4 cloves of garlic, basil, or if not available, marjoram or parsley, Dutch cheese and parmesan, grate them together, then grind the mixture in a mortar until it is reduced to a paste. Dilute it with an abundance of (olive oil).*

Not a pine nut in sight!

Pesto is dead! Long live Pesto!

cipolle ripiene in verde
baked red onions filled with pesto & ricotta

While stuffed antipasto vegetables are the preserve of Puglia, Piedmont is king when it comes to stuffing red onions. Breadcrumbs, *amaretto*, *mostarda*, hazelnuts, parmesan and meat are all employed to this end. The pairing of ricotta and pesto suggests we have nevertheless crossed the border into Liguria for simpler delights!

Serves 4
Preparation 40 minutes
Cooking time 30 minutes

4 large red onions
3 tbsp, 50g, 1/4 cup Dress Italian Basil Pesto
200g, 7oz, 1/2 cup fresh ricotta
4 tbsp, 60 ml, 2fl oz extra virgin olive oil
salt and black pepper

Preheat the oven to 220 C, 425 F, Gas mark 7

Peel the red onions and cook in boiling water for 10 minutes. Slice about 2cm off the top of each onion. Scoop out the inside with a spoon keeping about 4 layers of the outside onion to make a shell. Mix the ricotta and Dress Italian Basil Pesto together and season to taste with salt and black pepper.

Fill each of the onions with ricotta and pesto mix and place on a greased baking tray. Bake for 25 minutes until the onions are cooked and the filling slightly bubbly.

Serve as a side vegetable or with a salad as a light lunch.

Coda:
The onions can be served hot or are equally delicious at room temperature.

carote e porri glassati al miele
glazed leeks & carrots

The theft of what we now refer to as 'poor man's asparagus' rated a pretty hefty fine in the Middle Ages, being equivalent to that for stealing a live chicken! The less insistent flavour of leeks together with the natural sweetness of baby carrots, blend famously under the judicial glaze of balsamic vinegar flavoured honey.

Serves 4
Preparation time 10 minutes
Cooking time 30 minutes

500g, 1lb leeks, cleaned and cut lengthways
500g, 1lb carrots peeled and cut lengthways
6 tbsp, 90ml, 3fl oz extra virgin olive oil
salt and freshly ground black pepper
2 tbsp Dress Italian Balsamic Honey Glaze

Preheat the oven to 220 C, 425 F, Gas mark 7

Place the leeks and carrots on a baking tray. Season with salt and pepper and pour over the extra virgin olive oil. Toss the vegetables so that they are all seasoned and lightly coated in the extra virgin olive oil.

Bake for about 25 minutes until cooked. Remove the vegetables from the oven, toss through Dress Italian Balsamic Honey Glaze and return to the oven for a final 3 minutes.

Serve either hot or at room temperature.

pere al vino rosso con crema di mascarpone

marinated pears in red wine with mascarpone cream

Marinating pears in Dress Italian Clementine Mostarda Marinade which includes ginger, lemon, olive oil and vinegar sounds audacious, but the utterly delicious result proves otherwise. As the last recipe in this book, it hopefully underlines that a little further knowledge about Italian food can engender a new spirit of rediscovery and informed experimentation.

Serves 4
Preparation time 30 minutes
Cooking time 40 minutes

4 firm pears, peeled
1 orange sliced (with peel)
8 tbsp, 140g, 1/2 cup Dress Italian Clementine Mostarda Marinade
4 tbsp castor sugar
600ml, 20fl oz, 1 pint, 2 1/2 cups red wine
6 juniper berries, lightly crushed
1/2 tsp cinnamon

for the mascarpone cream
3 egg yolks
3 tbsp sugar
300ml whipping cream
300g mascarpone
3 tbsp Marsala

Marinate the pears in Dress Italian Clementine Mostarda for at least 20 minutes. Place the pears in a heavy based saucepan and pour over the red wine, orange slices, sugar, juniper berries and cinnamon. Simmer gently for 30 minutes ensuring that the liquid does not evaporate.

Meanwhile, beat the egg yolks and sugar together for 5 minutes. Add the whipping cream, mascarpone and *Marsala* and continue to beat for a further 3 - 5 minutes or until the cream has thickened.

Remove the pears with a slotted spoon, set aside and keep warm. Turn the heat up and reduce the red wine to a syrupy consistency. Serve the pears warm, drizzled with red wine syrup and a generous spoonful of mascarpone cream.

glossary of Italian references

Agrodolce   Sweet & sour flavouring of meats, fish and vegetables using vinegar and sugar.   Popularised during the Renaissance, it is still very much used in southern Italy.

Al forno   Roasted or baked in the oven.

Al modo mio   In my way.

All'agro   A lemon juice and oil dressing for vegetables or fish.

Anatra   Duck.

Arrangiarsi   The art of making do.

Baccalá   Salted cod.   Once caught, the cod is salted on board boats and dried when the fisherman come back to port.   It is soaked in several changes of water for up to 24 hours.   It can be prepared in a number of ways and differs from region to region.

Béchamel   See Besciamella.

Besciamella Sauce   Béchamel, A traditional white sauce served with vegetables or fish or for use as a basis for other sauces.
To make 1.2 litres, take 1.2 litres milk, 1/2 onion, 1/2 carrot, 1-2 parsley sprigs, 1-2 thyme sprigs, 2 bay leaves, 2-3 blades mace, 6 peppercorns, 1/2 x 5ml spoon salt, 50g butter, 50g plain flour.

Method: Put the milk in a saucepan with the onion, carrot, herbs and seasonings.   Heat gently just to scalding point, then remove from heat, cover and leave to infuse for 20 minutes.   Strain.   Melt the butter in a pan, add the flour and cook, stirring for 2 minutes, Remove from the heat and stir in the milk.   Return to the heat and cook, stirring for 5 minutes.

Braciola   Chop or cutlet, usually pork but also lamb, beef or game.

Brasato   Braised, often in Barolo wine.

Brodetto   A thick fish soup typical of the Marche region.   In Ancona, a traditional brodetto can contain up to 13 types of regional fish from the Adriatic sea often cooked in a tomato and garlic base.

Calda/Caldo   Hot.

Canederli   Gnocchi type dumpling typical of Trentino-Alto Adige.   It is made with eggs, stale bread, flour, milk, speck, onion and herbs.   The dough is shaped to resemble gnocchi and cooked in stock.

Caponata   A Sicilian vegetable dish made of (usually) deep fried aubergines (eggplant), celery, capers, anchovies, chilli, olives, tomatoes, vinegar and onions.   Traditional versions may also contain sultanas and pine nuts.

Capriolo   Venison or roe deer.

Carré d'Agnello   Roast loin or saddle of lamb.

Cavolo nero   Dark green cabbage. typical of Tuscany, closely related to curly kale.   Cavolo nero is shredded and sautéed as a side dish to meats or added to thick bean soups.

Cipolle   Onions.

Cipolline   Small or baby white onions; pearl onions

Chianina   A Tuscan breed of beef from the Val di Chianina

Con   With.

Crescenza   Soft, mild, creamy cow's milk cheese from Lombardy, aged for 15 days then shaped into slabs.   Delicious both as it is or heated although it does tend to 'run' as a result.

Crudo   Raw or rare.   In the case of prosciutto it means 'cured' raw meat.

Di   Of.

Fichi   Figs.

Finto (Farsu)   False, fake, pretend; sugo finto is the paupers' ragù made with pork fat instead of meat.

Frittata   Omelette like dish filled with vegetables or ham either sautéed or baked.

Funghi   Mushrooms.

Gamberi   Shrimps or prawns. Gamberetti are very small prawns whereas Gamberoni are very large prawns.

Già bagnato   Already wet or moistened.

Glassati   Glazed.

Grappa   A distilled spirit made from fermented grape pomace.   It is made by combining equal volumes of pomace and water in a copper pot for distillation.

Imbottiti   Literally: to put in barrels or fill.

glossary

In cartoccio In foil: something baked wrapped in foil.
In verde Literally: in green.
Infilzate On a skewer.
Insalata Salad. A generic term for salad or salad leaves.
Involtini Any food rolled or stuffed, usually fish or meat.
Linguine Thin, flat pasta ribbons. Literally means 'little tongues'.
Lombo Loin of meat, usually pork or beef.
Mafalda bread Braided semolina flour bread from Sicily topped with sesame seeds.
Magra Thin or lean. Refers to dishes that are usually meatless to adhere to Catholic fasting days.
Maiale Pork, the principal meat of the Italian diet. *Porchetta* is a whole roasted suckling pig wheras *Arista* refers to boneless roast pork.
Manzo Beef, usually refers to steers of 4 years or older.
Marsala An Italian wine fortified from the town of Marsala in western Sicily.
Mazzancolle Large Mediterranean prawns or shrimps.
Melanzane Aubergine or eggplant.
Merluzzo Fresh cod. *Merluzzo bianco* refers to Atlantic cod whereas *baccalà* refers to the salted cod.
Miele Honey.
Morbido Soft or tender.
Mostarda A sweet and sour chutney-like condiment made from candied fruits or vegetables preserved in a mustard syrup. Traditionally used as an accompaniment to boiled meats.
Orzo Barley. *Orzo perlato* is pearl barley.
Orzotto A risotto-like dish made with pearl barley instead of rice.
Pappardelle Literally: 'Gulp down'. Broad, flat ribbon-like pasta. Traditionally served in Tuscany with a hare ragù.
Pasticcio The art of creating something from ingredients at hand into a presentable dish. Literally: 'A mess'. *Un bel pasticcio* translates as "a fine mess"

Pellegrino Artusi Renowned 19th century Italian chef credited with writing the first complete Italian cookbook.
Pepe Pepper.
Peperonata A sauté or stew of sweet peppers, olive oil and garlic. The Italian answer to ratatouille.
Pere Pears.
Petto (di Pollo) Breast (of Chicken).
Piedmont DOP Cheeses Cheese produced only in the Piedmont region and protected by the Denominazione Origine Produzione. These include Bra, Castelmagno, Gorgonzola, Grana Padano, Murazzano, Raschera, Robiola di Roccaverano.
Pilaf rice Method of cooking rice so that every grain remains separate. Usually served with a meat dish.
Pinoli Pine nuts from the Italian stone pine tree. Important in Liguria for use in pesto, also in Sicily when combined with sultanas or raisins.
Pizza Arguably Neapolitan in origin, where the best pizzas are still to be had. None better than that to be experienced at Pizzeria da Michele, in Naples.
Pollo Chicken.
Polpette Meatballs.
Porri Leeks.
Portafoglio 'Wallet' or pocket sliced into meats.
Prosciutto di San Daniele Less salty than Parma ham, this prosciutto is from the area surrounding the town of San Daniele del Friuli. It is recognisable as the pig's trotter is usually still attached.
Quaglie Quail.
Radicchio Type of chicory with either red, purple or green leaves. Eaten either raw in salads or grilled and topped with mozzarella.
Rucola Rocket, arugula. Very peppery salad leaf often found growing wild in Italy.
Salsa madre The 'mother' sauce, usually tomato based, from which other sauces can be derived.
Saltati (in Padella) Sauté in a pan.

glossary

Scottato Seared or blanched, cooked very quickly.

Sfizio Little appetisers, accompaniments or snacks.

Saor Method of marinating in a sweet-sour combination. Orginated in Venice where they use a sweet vinegar, onion, sultanas and pine nuts marinade for fish, in particular, sardines.

Sofegao Literally: suffocated. Cooking something in a very small amount of liquid, usually in a covered pan.

Spiedini Food on a skewer, usually cooked over a fire.

Spigola/Branzino Seabass. Neapolitans refer to it as spigola whereas it is known throughout Italy as branzino.

Stoccafisso Air dried cod, unsalted. *Stoccafisso Accomodato* is flavoured with olives, anchovies, potatoes and pine nuts.

Strangolaprete Literally: 'priest chokers'. A type of flour and water pasta. In Naples it is small gnocchi.

Sugo finto Literally: false sauce. A meatless but satisfying pasta sauce often made with pork fat instead of meat.

Tagliata Fine slices of meat, usually served rare.

Timballo Dish that has been formed into a mould. Aubergine is often used as the 'pastry' and filled with vegetables, meat or pasta.

Tomini Small fresh cow's or goat's milk cheese traditionally from Piedmont.

Tonnara Name given to Sicilian tuna fishing fleets.

Tortine Small pies or flans usually made from vegetables.

Ubriache Literally: drunken. Refers to ingredients cooked in a large amount of wine.

Ventresca The preserved belly of the tuna.

Verdure Vegetables.

Zucchine Courgettes.

Zuppa Thick soup, usually served with bread.

DRESS
Italian

L'ORIENTALE
dressing

EXTRA VIRGIN OLIVE OIL

FIGS

list of recipes

antipasti

primi piatti

pesce

carne

rack of lamb with garlic and rosemary 71
pork cutlets with l'orientale mash 72
marinated duck breast with pears 74
braised lamb shanks with red wine 76
pork wrapped in pancetta with a mascarpone stuffing 78
aubergine parcels filled with meatballs 83
warm salad with chicken, figs and radicchio 85
pork cutlets with sweet and sour sauce 86
baked chicken with apricots, prunes and couscous 88-89
beef fillet with black olives 93
marinated venison with red cabbage 95
roasted quail on a bed of saffron risotto 99
marinated chicken with black cabbage 100
baked gammon and pears in red wine 102
barbecued, skewered beef 105
stir fry of duck breast and bok choy 106

verdure

caramelised baby onions 109
stuffed baked peppers 111
gorgonzola, pear and pine nut salad 113
baked red onions filled with pesto and ricotta 116
glazed leeks and carrots 118

dolci

marinated pears in red wine with mascarpone cream 120